# Fair play

It is never too early to teach your child about playing fair. Take advantage of opportunities at home to encourage respect for other family members; to learn to share toys; to be nice, and patient, and to take turns.

In other words praise your child for fair play.

Praising effort is important, particularly when young children are still developing skills such as running, jumping and coordination. Success should be based on joining in and trying, rather than 'being the best' as only one person can be the best.

Let's encourage fair play with our children. Being a good role model is important, whether you are actively involved in the game or just watching. If you are polite and respectful, both 'on the field and off the field', your child is more likely to develop the same attitudes.

Mentioning the words fair play as often as possible will help your child to understand what it means from this early stage.

1

# Bookbug

Bookbug encourages parents, carers and children to read and sing together from birth. We give books to every child in Scotland in four age-appropriate Bookbug Bags.

- **Bookbug Baby Bag** (given by your health visitor when your baby is between 3 and 5 weeks old)
- **Bookbug Toddler Bag** (given by your health visitor when your toddler is aged between 13 and 15 months)
- **Bookbug Explorer Bag** (given at nursery when your child is 3)
- **Bookbug Primary 1 Family Bag** (given at school when your child is in P1)

If you haven't received your free Bookbug Toddler Bag, please ask your health visitor for more details.

Families can also have Gaelic versions of the bags as well as their English versions. We can also provide tactile books for children and families with additional support needs.

Come along to free Bookbug Sessions at your local library or community group. These are free, fun sessions of stories, songs and rhymes to enjoy with your child and other families. Find your nearest Bookbug Session at **www.scottishbooktrust.com/localbookbugsessions** or ask at your local library.

Bookbug is run by Scottish Book Trust and funded by the Scottish Government and Creative Scotland. Local Bookbug activity is coordinated by the library or education service together with the NHS. Find out more at **www.scottishbooktrust.com/bookbug**.

# Contents

# The importance of play@home

The first seven years of life are the most influential in establishing good exercise habits and setting the foundation for learning throughout life. Everything children do is exercise related, whether it is talking (exercising the jaw and brain) or walking. Having daily exercise routines at an early age helps children to become strong and healthy as they grow. This develops their self-esteem and encourages them to 'have a go' at new activities.

It is important for parents and carers to be active with their children, not only as role models, but also for their own health and energy. This provides the foundation for a physically active life for the whole family, and encourages enjoyment of physical activities, sport and exercise.

Note
For ease of reading and not to show any preference, we use both his and her throughout the programme. For children with additional needs some of these activities may need to be adapted. Discuss this with your child's therapist.

# Benefits of play@home

This book:

- Encourages you to establish daily health-related routines with your toddler.

- Encourages you as parents and carers to become your children's first teachers.

- Encourages your toddler's enjoyment of physical activity which will lead to a healthier life.

- Develops body awareness and promotes the development of good patterns of movement.

- Promotes the value of finding playmates for your toddler, so that they learn to interact and think about others.

- Encourages communication through talking and listening.

- Stimulates your toddler's curiosity, imagination and creativity.

- Promotes the value of giving praise and positive reassurance.

- Encourages good loving touch in your family and strengthens parent/child relationships.

- Promotes the value of you, the parent, doing daily exercise as a role model for your toddler.

# How to use your play@home toddler programme

- Begin by reading the section 'Facts about toddlers' and then the purple 12–18 months section.

- Move on to the next section, orange, 18 months–2 years, when you think your toddler is ready.

- Remember that all toddlers are different and have their own timetable of development. Some will enjoy activities beyond the stated age group, others will not be ready to do some things at the stated time.

- As your toddler progresses, move on to the blue 2–2$\frac{1}{2}$ years section, and finally the green 2$\frac{1}{2}$–3 years section.

- Choose what your toddler likes and what suits your family situation from the selection of activities.

- Use the ideas in this book as starting points for your own ideas. Make up your own games, invent your own toys. Share your ideas and discoveries with others.

- If you are unsure about the suitability of a toy for a particular age, give your toddler one which is a little too difficult rather than one which is too simple. Toys which are too easy are quickly discarded.

# Facts about toddlers

## Development and play

Your child never stops developing. The order of development is the same in all children, but the rate of development varies from child to child. For example, a toddler needs to learn to walk before learning to run, but the age at which toddlers learn to walk and to run varies considerably.

Play and play materials have educational value, and are part of the basic needs of all toddlers to help them in their stages of development. Play also keeps them occupied and prevents boredom which quickly leads to frustration and bad temper. You should provide toddlers with play activities suitable for their individual stages of development and those which are interesting to them, remembering that toys which interest one child will not necessarily interest another.

Play helps toddlers to discover, practise and develop new and old skills, to concentrate, to experiment and to use their imagination. It gives them emotional satisfaction and a sense of achievement. Play is the basis of their learning.

Note
If you feel your toddler is not progressing as expected and you think there could be something wrong, contact your health visitor or doctor.

## Social interaction

Toddlers enjoy playing alongside others of similar ages, although each of them will be involved in separate activities. The first stage in learning about socialising is when they begin to develop an awareness of other people's reactions to them, together with the give and take necessary for group life. Parallel play gives them the opportunity to discover that they are like other children, concerned with the same things and that they do many things as well as others, perhaps some things better. This develops self-confidence. Playing alongside others enables toddlers to explore the possibilities of their world and their own potential as individuals.

## Nutrition

Toddlers require good food and regular small snacks because they are very active and growing fast. Eating habits vary enormously from one child to another – some eat like birds and others have ravenous appetites. It is important to provide them with healthy foods with all the nutrients they need, so that they begin to learn good eating habits at home. For information about healthy meals and snacks for toddlers and the whole family contact your health visitor.

## Language development

Toddlers learn to communicate by listening and concentrating when someone is talking. It is just as important for your toddler to understand language as it is for them to actually speak it. It is important to talk to toddlers directly so that they can see facial expressions and gestures. The conversation needs to relate to what is happening now (such as eating, dressing, playing), or to what is going to happen: 'We are going to visit Grandma'. Toddlers need to be listened to when they are trying to communicate, showing them that what they have to say is important and interesting. Praise or positive reassurance with all their efforts, no matter how small, encourages them to continue their learning.

## Books

Books are important in development of the language skills of listening, understanding and communicating. Reading books with your toddler helps to develop their visual understanding and the ability to notice detail, and stimulate the imagination. An early enjoyment of books provides a foundation for a child's more formal education later on. Toddlers should not be forced to look at books when they would clearly prefer to be doing something else, but by seeing adults enjoy and care for books, they learn by example. Books, magazines, newspapers and comics should all be seen around the home as valued and looked after. Toddlers should be encouraged to copy adults even before they can read.

## Toddler behaviour

Toddler behaviour is very confusing because their desire for independence conflicts with their desire for emotional support. They often do not know what they want, so can't make decisions easily, and will change their mind several times.

They will often fight against control and help, and insist on doing things for themselves (like dressing) even though they are unable to do so. On the other hand toddlers also depend on you totally for emotional support. They will cling to you, cry when you leave the room and hold their arms up to be carried.

Toddlers will sometimes be selfish, which is important for defining who they are and to understand their relationship to things and people. They like to play by themselves, and will often play alongside other children with little interaction apart from a tug-of-war over a toy. Sharing can't be rushed, but toddlers need to be given plenty of opportunities to learn to share and to take turns.

Toddlers need to learn for themselves what is appropriate behaviour and need your love and approval to be adventurous and try out new activities in their own environment.

# Play materials

Cheap materials have been used in nearly all the activities in this book, most of which you'll have in your home. Some items can be used in lots of different ways, so you won't have to go out and buy a lot of things to clutter your cupboards and shelves. The most expensive toys are not always the best toys, and because they're expensive doesn't mean that your toddler will prefer them.

Household items to save:

- empty plastic bottles that have not contained poisonous or harmful substances
- large bottle caps, egg boxes
- cardboard boxes of all sizes
- foil
- old magazines, newspapers and junk mail
- kitchen towel tubes
- string and wool
- paper, corks
- material scraps, cotton reels.

Environmental items to collect include shells, dried leaves, acorns, pine cones and so on.

Pages 12 to 18 include instructions and recipes for play materials that have been suggested in some of the play@home toddler activities.

# How to make a pom-pom

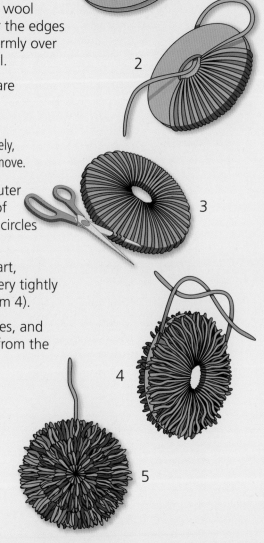

- To make a pom-pom, first cut two circles out of a piece of cardboard, and then cut the centres out of each circle (see diagram 1).

- Place the two circles together, one on top of the other.

- Thread a double length of wool through the hole and over the edges (see diagram 2), binding firmly over the loose ends of the wool.

- Continue until the circles are completely covered.

Note:
Do not fill up the centre hole entirely, or the circles will be difficult to remove.

- Cut the wool round the outer edge, inserting the point of your scissors between the circles (see diagram 3).

- Ease the circles slightly apart, and tie a length of wool very tightly between them (see diagram 4).

- Pull off the cardboard circles, and trim off any uneven ends from the pom-pom.

- The finished pom-pom (see diagram 5).

# How to make a bean bag

- Cut out two pieces of fabric approximately 14 cm x 20 cm.

- Place the right sides of the fabric together and sew around the edges with a 1.5 cm seam, leaving a 5 cm opening along one side.

- Turn the fabric through the hole so that the right sides show, and iron it.

- Sew around the bag as close to the edge as possible.

- Fill it with approximately two cups of uncooked rice, and then close the opening with two rows of stitching. (Dried peas, beans, lentils or sand can be used instead).

Bean bags can be thrown, balanced on your head or slid along the floor.

## How to make a music shaker

- Use small boxes, plastic bottles or containers (clear or coloured).

- Part fill with lentils, beans, rice or broth mix.

- Make sure shaker is securely fastened.

0

5 cm

10 cm

14 cm

## Playdough (uncooked)

- 1$\frac{1}{4}$ cups flour
- $\frac{1}{2}$ cup salt
- $\frac{1}{2}$ cup water
- Combine the flour and salt and slowly mix in the water.
- Work the mixture into a smooth dough with your fingers.

## Playdough (cooked)

- 2 cups plain flour
- 1 cup salt
- 2 teaspoons cream of tartar
- 1 tablespoon cooking oil
- 2 cups cold water
- A few drops of food colouring, depending on the colour you want.
- Place all ingredients except water and food colouring into a large bowl. Fill cup with water, add food colouring, gradually add to ingredients in the bowl, mixing well, then add second cup of water in the same way. Give a good whisk.

This mixture can be cooked in two ways:

## Pan

- Pour the mixture into a large saucepan and cook over a low heat, stirring often with a strong metal spoon to prevent sticking on the bottom and to help even cooking.

- When the mixture has cooked and formed into a solid ball, remove from the heat. *Tip mixture onto a work surface, allow to cool slightly, then knead like bread dough for around two minutes. The dough is now ready to use. Store in an airtight container in the fridge. It should keep for a few weeks.

## Microwave

- Place bowl of whisked ingredients into the microwave (remember to remove metal spoon or whisk), and cook on full power for around two minutes. Carefully remove from microwave and stir. Return to the microwave for about one minute, then repeat stirring and cooking until dough appears cooked. Make sure there is no uncooked dough but be careful not to over cook. Proceed as from *pan cooking method.

## Variations

- To make your playdough a bit more interesting or to change the texture, add macaroni, glitter, oatmeal, colourings or scented flavourings.

## Homemade glue recipes

- 1 cup water

- 1 heaped teaspoon flour

- Mix the flour to a paste with a little water, then add the rest of the water and boil the mixture for a few minutes. Cool in a covered container.

# Homemade paint recipes

Here are three different recipes to choose from:

1. Beat together soap flakes and warm water to make a mixture that looks like whipped potatoes. Add food colouring of your choice.

2. 1 cup cornflour
   1 cup soap flakes
   1 litre boiling water
   food colouring

   Dissolve the cornflour in a little cold water. Slowly add the boiling water and boil until thick. Take it off the heat and beat in the soap flakes. Add food colouring.

3. 1 cup flour
   3 cups boiling water
   1 cup cold water
   food colouring
   $1/4$ teaspoon dishwashing detergent

   Combine the flour, detergent and cold water, stirring until it is smooth. Gradually pour the mixture into the boiling water and bring it to the boil, stirring constantly. Add food colouring and let it cool.

Note
These recipes can be used for either finger painting or brush painting. Store the paint in airtight containers. The paints made with soap flakes are easier to wash off clothes and surfaces.

# Homemade bubbles recipes

### Bubbles

Mix together:

18 fl oz water

2 fl oz washing-up liquid

4 teaspoons sugar

food colouring (optional)

### Longer lasting bubbles

Mix together:

6 fl oz water

2 fl oz washing-up liquid

2 fl oz glycerine

1 tablespoon sugar

### Frothy bubbles

For frothy bubbles mix washing-up liquid and water, or bubble bath and water, in a small bowl. Blow bubbles through a straw in the bowl. For coloured bubbles add some food colouring.

Remember:
Do not let your toddler swallow the bubbles.

# section 1

## 12–18 months

**Bookbug says:**
Bring your toddler along to fun, free Bookbug Sessions for stories, songs and rhymes at your local library. To find details of your local session go to **www.scottishbooktrust.com/ localbookbugsessions**

# Loving touch

## Instructions

- Massage your toddler whenever you get the opportunity.

- It is not too late to start massage with your toddler. (See pages 170–177)

- Make the most of times when your toddler is looking at books or playing quietly to lovingly stroke his hair and shoulders, and massage his feet.

## Variations

- Try soothing your toddler with loving cuddles and relaxing hair and back rubs when he's upset, angry, ill or tired.

- Take the opportunity to massage his legs, feet and each tiny toe during nappy changing times. Include rhymes or songs, such as This little piggy went to market.

## Precautions

- Do not expect your toddler to sit still in one place for a period of time, make the most of opportunities to massage as they occur.

- Using oil may be more of a danger than a help now, making him very slippery to handle if active.

# benefits

- Physical – Toning skin and muscles and encouraging relaxation.
- Other – Developing body awareness and enhancing parent/child relationship.

# Stand and walk

## Instructions

- Teach your toddler to walk sideways and backwards with one or both hands held.
- Stand up a distance away and encourage her to walk and then run up to you.

## Variations

- Teach her to turn around in a circle and walk around obstacles like a chair.
- Provide her with a large wheeled toy that she can push and pull.
- Encourage her to squat down and pick up a toy off the floor and stand up again with a helping hand.
- Help her to learn to walk up and down stairs (see Baby Book, 10–12 months), and to walk on different surfaces; concrete, sand, uneven ground, and so on.
- Let her learn by watching children and adults moving.

## Precautions

- Provide an obstacle-free area for her to practise walking and running.
- Ensure that her play area is safe to protect her from injury.

- Do not worry if your toddler doesn't want to walk yet. Go back to the walking exercise in the 10–12 months section of your play@home Baby Book.

- Babywalkers will disrupt the natural pattern of your child's development and are not recommended by experts.

Suggested rhyme – Ring a ring o'roses (page 193)

# benefits

- **Physical – Developing balance, coordination and movement skills.**
- **Other – Gaining a sense of achievement in discovering new capabilities. Practising judging distances.**

# Animal sounds

## Instructions

- Find a book with large pictures of farm animals from the library, a friend or a bookshop.
- Sit together and look at the book.
- Point to an animal, name it, and then make the sound the animal makes. Move on to the next animal in the book and repeat.
- Encourage your toddler to copy your words, sounds and facial expressions.

## Variations

- Find different books such as a transport book with trucks, planes and motorbikes, or a book of zoo animals.
- Make your own picture books with a scrap book, using magazine pictures and your own drawings and make up a story.

## Precaution

- Toddlers experiment with the feel and sound of tearing paper, so keep delicate books out of reach and provide him with a variety of books with cardboard or fabric pages for him to help himself to.

Suggested rhyme – Baa baa black sheep (page 180)

# benefits

- Physical – Encouraging relaxation and using pictures to learn about movement.
- Other – Developing vocabulary and learning about animals. Encouraging an enjoyment of books.

# Follow the ball

## Instructions

- Roll a lightweight ball across the grass and encourage your toddler to get it and bring it to you.
- Roll the ball in different directions each time and encourage her to follow.
- Repeat this until you have had enough.

## Variations

- Vary the size of the ball.
- Vary the surfaces to roll the ball over.
- Roll the ball at different speeds for her to chase.
- Teach her to roll or throw the ball back to you.
- Include other children in the game so that she can watch how they handle the ball.
- Let her watch a dog play the same game.

Adapt this game for inside play.

## Precaution

- Make sure the play area is fenced so that your toddler can't chase the ball onto the road.

 # benefits

- Physical – Developing movement skills, balance, flexibility and hand/eye coordination. Learning to follow objects with her eyes.
- Other – Exploring space and movement of objects. Socialising and interacting skills.

# Music fun

## Instructions

- Turn on some music, sing along and encourage your toddler to copy you.
- Hold your toddler's hands and dance around.
- Clap to the music and encourage him to copy you.
- Pick him up and rock him to the beat of the music.

## Variations

- Use a homemade shaker. (see page 13)
- Hum, whistle or sing your own songs.
- Tell simple nursery rhymes and clap your hands or stamp your foot to the rhythm, for example:

  Pat-a-cake, pat-a-cake, baker man,

  Bake me a cake as fast as you can.

  Pat it and prick it and mark it with B,

  Put it in the oven for baby and me.

- Let him make his own 'music' during play such as banging a wooden spoon on a saucepan, or tapping a pencil on a box.

# benefits

Your toddler will enjoy making spontaneous music by experimenting with sounds which he will repeat again and again.

- Physical – Achieving balance and coordination. Developing a sense of rhythm.
- Other – Learning by observing. Imitating and experimenting with sounds. Learning new words.

# Follow me

## Instructions

- Tie a piece of wool through a cotton reel, for your toddler to pull.
- Encourage her to pull it along the floor on carpet, lino, concrete, grass, dirt and other surfaces.
- Drop the reel over the side of a chair, or into a box, and give her the end of the wool to pull it back up with.

## Variations

- As she watches, hide the reel under a pillow or inside a container with the end of the wool visible so that she can pull it out.
- Tie the wool around other objects such as an egg box, an empty plastic bottle, a rattle, a plastic kitchen utensil, or something that she is particularly interested in at the moment.
- Tie the wool around something that floats for her to pull around the bath or in a bowl of water.

## Precaution

- Supervise all play with wool because there is a risk that she may wind it around her neck.

Suggested rhyme – One two three four five (page 191)

 **benefits**

- **Physical – Developing grasp and hand/eye coordination. Exercising her whole body.**
- **Other – Experimenting with weight, gravity, sound and friction. Learning new words.**

# Meal time

## Instructions

- Provide an extra teaspoon at mealtimes for your toddler to learn to hold and to attempt to feed himself.
- Put food on his spoon and encourage him to take it to his mouth.
- Praise his efforts each time he tries, even when he misses his mouth.

## Variations

- Give him a cup to drink from and plenty of help. Encourage him to use both hands.
- Give him finger foods like little sandwiches or crackers and let him feed himself.

## Precautions

- It will take a lot of practice for him to learn how to feed himself, and a lot of patience and support from you.
- To avoid mess from spillages, cover the floor under the highchair with newspaper or plastic.
- Don't give him raisins, whole grapes or nuts as he could choke on them.

Suggested rhyme – Ten fat sausages (page 195)

 # benefits

- Physical – Developing hand/eye and hand/mouth coordination. Learning fine movement skills.
- Other – Learning by observing, thinking and experimenting. Asserting independence.

# Snack time

## Instructions

- Let your toddler try different foods for a snack.

- Provide a choice of hot and cold, smooth and lumpy, wet and dry food, for example, spaghetti hoops, crisps, cheese puffs, custard, rice pudding, bread, plain pasta shapes, jelly.

- Encourage him to explore the texture by taste and touch.

- Allow him to make a mess.

## Variations

- Give him the chance to use both hands.

- Allow him to feed you, or his dolly.

## Precautions

- Supervise him when eating.

- Avoid nuts, whole grapes and raisins as he may choke on them.

Suggested rhyme – Jelly on a plate (page 189)

 # benefits

- Physical – Hand/eye coordination. Learning to chew.
- Other – Showing that food is fun. Exploring textures and tastes. Developing lip and tongue movements.

# Falling object

## Instructions

- Drop some leaves in front of your toddler so that he can watch them fall to the ground.

- Now give him the leaves and let him drop them himself. Repeat several times.

- Provide a variety of objects that will fall in different ways such as a ball, stick, bean bag (see page 13), hat, sock, plastic bottle, soft toy, ribbon, balloon.

- Talk about what you are doing.

## Variations

- Vary the dropping height.

- Fill a bowl with water, or visit a lake, pond or the beach and drop stones, sand, leaves, driftwood and bread for the birds into the water.

- Give him the chance to hold and drop the objects with both left and right hands.

- Your toddler will also enjoy dropping objects from his highchair or cot onto the floor.

## Precaution

- Check he's only dropping objects that you want him to drop.

Suggested rhyme – Humpty Dumpty (page 186)

# benefits

- **Physical – Developing hand/eye coordination. Learning how to grasp objects.**
- **Other – Learning about weight, gravity and movement of different objects when dropped. Learning new words.**

# Make it fit

## Instructions

- Make or buy a set of nesting toys; about six items of different sizes which fit inside each other.

- Show your toddler how they all fit together and then let him tip them all out and try to imitate you.

- Repeat this again and again until he has had enough.

## Variations

- Find some containers with lids that your toddler can take off and put on, and objects he can put inside the containers.

- Provide postbox toys that have different shaped holes and shapes to fit in the hole. You can make your own by cutting out shapes in the lid of a cardboard box to post objects such as a small ball, a box or a cotton reel.

- Give him a large box with three or four different sized holes that he can choose to drop his toys through.

Note
Some toddlers prefer to be climbing, running and exploring rather than sitting, so don't be disappointed if he's not interested in this game for long – try again later on.

Suggested rhyme – Clap, clap hands (page 180)

# benefits

- Physical – Developing hand skills, hand/eye coordination and encouraging concentration.
- Other – Experimenting with size and shape. Learning about patience and trying things again and learning new words.

# Drawing

## Instructions

- Give your toddler large pieces of paper and two or three large, thick crayons to experiment with.
- Scribble with him watching.
- Let him scribble and jab with the crayon in his own style and with both left and right hands, holding the crayon whichever way he chooses.

## Variations

- Blackboard and thick chalk.
- Whiteboard and erasable marker.
- Finger paints (see recipes page 17).

Provide plenty of paper such as cardboard, wallpaper, newspapers and brown paper bags split open and laid flat.

## Precaution

- Make sure that the crayons and chalk are not small enough to choke on.

 # benefits

- Physical – Developing grasp, hand/eye coordination, and encouraging relaxation.
- Other – Discovering new capabilities, new words and colours. Learning by example.

# Messy play

## Instructions

- Use finger paints (see page 17 for recipe).
- Sit your toddler in her chair with a tray in front.
- Remove or protect her clothes.
- Put blobs of paint on the tray (2–3 colours).
- Show her how to spread the paint using her whole hand.
- Allow her plenty of time to make a mess.
- Have a damp cloth and towel ready to wipe clean.

## Variations

Try this with yogurt, custard, cornflour mixed with water, jelly, rice pudding. Try different temperatures – warm (not hot) custard. Drive a toy car through the mess.

Note
You can make a print of her patterns by laying a piece of paper over the paint on the tray.

# benefits

- Physical – Developing hand/eye coordination and hand movement skills.

- Other – Enjoying new sensations and textures. Discovering patterns. Teaching her that there is a time for messy play.

# Let's build

## Instructions

- Provide your toddler with a set of blocks to play with (these can be homemade using wood or cardboard).
- Build a tower with the blocks, let her knock them down, then rebuild them for her again and again.
- Encourage her to build up the blocks herself.
- Talk about what you are doing.

## Variations

- Try different objects for building with, such as empty cereal boxes and egg boxes, or plastic boxes from the kitchen cupboard.
- Stack cushions and pillows on top of each other.
- Smooth wooden offcuts can be stacked up outside and knocked over again.

## Precautions

- Your toddler may only be able to build up a tower of three blocks by the time she reaches eighteen months – but she will really enjoy knocking down whatever you build.
- Make sure wooden blocks are untreated, the edges are sanded and, if painted, use non-toxic paint.

Suggested rhyme – Jack and Jill (page 189)

 # benefits

- Physical – Developing hand skills, grasp and hand/ eye coordination. Experimenting with movement and balance.

- Other – Learning about size, shape, weight and gravity. Encouraging her to think and learn new words.

# Hide and seek

## Instructions

- Hide a toy under a cushion while your toddler watches, and then encourage him to find the toy. Repeat this several times.

- Hide different toys and objects under the cushion.

- Now encourage him to hide things under the cushion for you to find.

- Talk about what you are doing.

## Variations

- Try different hiding places such as in one of your hands, in a box, under an upturned bowl, behind your back, or in your pocket.

- Hide larger objects outside such as a large ball under a tree, behind a wall, or in a box.

Note
Start this game very simply by letting your toddler see where you hide the object and keep using that hiding place until he begins to understand the game.

He will become frustrated if you play this game for too long when he wants to play with the object you're hiding.

Suggested rhyme – Two little dicky birds (page 200)

 **benefits**

- Physical – Developing hand/eye coordination and movement skills.
- Other – Encouraging him to think and develop memory skills. Learning by example.

# Empty and fill

## Instructions

- Fill an old shopping bag or brown paper bag with all sorts of objects from your cupboards such as a wooden spoon, plastic egg cup, an old toothbrush, pegs, lids, a comb and some toys your toddler hasn't seen for a while.

- Let him spend time unpacking the items one by one, putting them all back in again and then tipping them out again.

- He will enjoy carrying his own shopping bag around with him too.

- He will enjoy the different feel of these objects.

## Variations

- Re-organise a kitchen cupboard with pots and pans and plastic containers for him to empty out and put away again.

- He will enjoy filling a wheelbarrow or box outside with toys, wood, garden utensils, leaves and so on and then emptying it again.

- Provide an old washing basket or box to use as a toy box to get things from whenever he chooses.

## Precautions

- Make sure the toys and objects will not cut, choke or cause other injuries to your toddler.

- Do not give him plastic bags.

- Put safety catches on doors and cupboards where you keep things that could hurt him.

# benefits

- **Physical – Developing grasp and hand/eye coordination.**
- **Other – Exploring the feel and shapes of objects. Developing curiosity and encouraging him to think.**

# Sand play

## Instructions

- Take your toddler to the beach to play.
- Allow her to walk barefoot on the sand.
- Let her play with wet and dry sand; feeling, sifting, moulding and digging.
- Find some shells to bury and sticks to dig with.
- Show her how to use a bucket and spade.
- Give her the opportunity to watch other children and adults playing on the beach.
- Talk about what you are doing and what you can see.

## Variations

- If it's warm enough take her down to the water to paddle, squeeze sand between her toes, and sit in a shallow rock pool.
- Build a sand pit in the garden to play in and invite other children to play in it with her.
- Set aside a dirt patch in the corner of the garden to play in if you don't have a sand pit.

## Precautions

- Always keep the sand pit or dirt patch covered when not in use to keep dogs and cats out.

- Supervise closely when walking barefoot.
- Supervise closely when near water.
- Put on sunblock and hat to avoid sunburn, and warm clothing on cold and windy days.

 # benefits

- **Physical – Developing hand skills, hand/eye coordination and balance. Exercising many different muscles.**
- **Other – Learning about textures, size and weight. Developing curiosity, imagination and vocabulary.**

# Let's exercise

## Instructions

- Do gentle exercises with your toddler.

- Arms: Lift them up above his head. Cross them over his chest. Raise one arm above the head and lie the other by his side, then change arms.

- Legs: Lying on his back with knees bent, place your hands flat on the soles of his feet and let him push against your hands. Hold his ankles and rotate his legs gently like riding a bicycle and then change direction.

## Variations

- Roly Poly: Lie him on a towel or blanket and roll him up like a Swiss roll, then unroll him, repeat if he enjoyed it.

- Tug of war: With him standing facing you, wrap a towel around his back and buttocks, and hold each end of the towel – encourage him to pull backwards away from you.

- Let him watch you exercising every day (like housework, aerobics, walking).

- Go to a toddler movement class.

## Precaution

- Be very gentle with the exercises, make sure that his limbs are relaxed before you move them in any direction, if not leave these exercises and play something else. Try them again another time.

Suggested rhyme – Head, shoulders, knees and toes (page 184)

 **benefits**

- **Physical – Developing movement skills and exercising different muscles.**
- **Other – Learning through watching and interaction, and using effort.**

# Let's climb

## Instructions

- Provide your toddler with a large cardboard box or the washing basket to climb in and out of.

- Teach him how to hold onto the sides, lift one leg over the side and then the other.

## Variations

- Teach him to climb over a low wall.

- Help him to climb onto a couch or bed and show him how to get back down again.

- Let him climb up and over you.

- Children's playgrounds and parks provide low obstacles for climbing into and over, and he can watch how other children climb.

- Ride-on toys are great for climbing on and off.

- Teach him to climb steps and come down again.

## Precautions

- If your toddler is likely to fall, make sure he will land on carpet or something soft.

- Supervise all climbing activities – he will want to climb everything and has no sense of danger. Teach him to climb up and down correctly. (See Baby Book, 10–12 months)

Suggested rhyme – Hey diddle diddle (page 185)

 **benefits**

- Physical – Developing balance, flexibility and coordination.
- Other – Exploring new activities and capabilities. Starting to understand height.

# Peek-a-boo

## Instructions

- Hide behind a door or a piece of furniture and call your toddler's name until he finds you and then say 'Boo'!
- Move to another hiding place with him following close behind, let him find you, and then say 'Boo'!
- Continue to find different places to hide.
- Let him hide and say 'Boo'!

## Variations

- Try the same activity outside in the garden, the park or a playground.
- Pretend to be an animal hiding, like a cat, so that when he finds you, you say 'meeow'.
- Hide under a box or a blanket for him to find you.

## Precautions

- Make sure your toddler has some idea of where you are all the time. Do this by calling him and allowing him to see where you're hiding. This means he won't get a fright and lose confidence.
- Make sure the play area is safe, to prevent injury.

 # benefits

- Physical – Developing balance and movement skills. Learning to react and move quickly.
- Other – Exploring space and the size of objects. Encouraging thinking and memory skills, learning new words.

# Autumn leaves

## Instructions

- Gather up a large pile of autumn leaves.
- Play together in the leaves with your toddler and other members of the family.
- Roll in them, throw them up in the air, catch them, hide under them.

## Variations

- Play inside or outside without the leaves; rolling and tumbling on the ground or floor, tickling and hugging.
- Put on old clothes and tumble in freshly mown grass clippings.
- Roll down small slopes together.
- Play in a ball pool.

## Precautions

- Make sure older children are not too lively.
- The play area needs to be free of danger, such as broken glass, dog mess, sharp objects.
- Be careful if there is a strong family history of allergies such as hayfever.

Suggested rhyme – One man went to mow (page 190)

 # benefits

- Physical – Developing movement skills, flexibility and coordination.
- Other – Learning by example and exploring new capabilities. Social interaction and learning new words.

# Water fun

## Instructions

- Fill a warm bath with a non-slip mat in the bottom for your toddler to play in.

- Give her things that float and some that sink, containers to pour with, and kitchen utensils to experiment with.

- Encourage her to kick and splash, and help her to float on her tummy and her back.

- Pour water down the back of her head, neck and shoulders, trickling a little over her face if she doesn't mind.

## Variations

- Make it a bubble bath.

- Fill a paddling pool outside, or give her a bucket or bowl of water to play with.

If you don't have a bath try filling a large bowl of water in the shower box.

## Precautions

- Never leave your toddler alone with water because she can drown in a very small amount in a very short time.

- Protect her from hot water and the hot tap to prevent burns.

- Don't persist with any water activity she dislikes. It may cause her to lose confidence.

Suggested rhyme – Five little ducks (page 182)

# benefits

- **Physical – Floating, kicking and splashing with resistance from the water. Good exercise for the whole body.**
- **Other – Gaining water confidence: the first stage of learning to swim. Learning new words. Measuring and pouring.**

# Balloons

## Instructions

- Blow up two or three brightly coloured balloons and tie a length of string around the end of each one.
- Hang them in a doorway or where your toddler can reach them.
- Hit the balloons up in the air for her to watch and then encourage her to join in and copy you.
- Other children can join in.

## Variations

- Teach her to hit the balloons with her head.
- Hang the balloons outside on the washing line so that she can watch and hit them as they blow in the wind.
- Try hanging several different objects at different heights such as soft toys.
- Give her a kitchen roll tube to bat the objects with.

## Precautions

- Watch your toddler when playing with string as there is a risk that she will become tangled in it.
- If a balloon bursts, collect up all the pieces so that your toddler doesn't choke on one.

- Make sure the outside play area is well fenced, so that if a balloon blows away your toddler won't come to any harm chasing it.

Suggested rhyme – Bell horses (page 180)

# benefits

- **Physical – Developing balance, upper body coordination, hand/eye coordination and flexibility. Exercising many different muscles.**
- **Other – Having fun and learning new words. Experimenting with weight and gravity. Socialising and interacting.**

# Pom-poms

## Instructions

- Make four or five pom-poms of different sizes, in bright colours. (see page 12)

- Tie each one to a length of wool and attach them to a hanger or stick so that they hang down.

- Hang them in the car in a position where your toddler can kick them with both feet.

## Variations

- Try using different items to hang up such as soft toys, rattles, or a cardboard tube covered with tinfoil.

- Hang them in front of the highchair or over the end or side of the cot and encourage her to kick them with her feet.

- When she's in the bath, help her to lie back, and encourage her to kick floating items such as toys, containers and sponges.

## Precautions

- When going out in the car always strap your toddler into a safe car seat. Contact your health visitor for information about car seats.

- Supervise bath play. Your toddler can drown in a small amount of water in a very short time.

 # benefits

- Physical – Developing lower body coordination.
- Other – Exploring new capabilities, having fun and preventing boredom in the car.

# section 2

## 18 months–2 years

**Bookbug says:**
Reading with your toddler doesn't have to take long. You just need a few minutes a day to share books together. Sit your child on your knee or close to you, and simply turn the pages of a book, chatting about the pictures.

# Cuddle fun

## Instructions

- Continue to provide plenty of loving touch and massage daily.
- When playing tig or hide and seek with your toddler: catch her, give her a big cuddle and then let her run away again.
- Repeat this several times.
- Then change places and let her catch and cuddle you.

## Variations

- Roll and tumble on the floor together, and take her for rides on your back.
- When changing her, or at bathtime, blow raspberries on her tummy, back, arms, legs and feet. Laugh and giggle together.
- Each night, give all members of the family a kiss and a hug before going to bed. Your toddler might like to do this with her stuffed toys and dolls too.

## Precautions

- Let her break contact when she wants to.
- Your toddler may become very excited during this game, so give her time to wind down afterwards with a quiet game or book.

Suggested rhyme – Two little hands (page 201)

 # benefits

- Physical – Combining loving touch with active play.
- Other – Learning by example and feeling good together.

# Go for a ride

## Instructions

- Find a cardboard box for your toddler to push around the floor.

- Put some toys or stuffed animals in the box and encourage him to take them for a ride in it.

- Add a few more items to the box to make it a little heavier, so that he uses more force to push it.

## Variations

- Replace the box with a trolley with wheels, doll's pram or pushchair for outside play.

- Tie some string to the box so that he can try pulling it around instead of pushing it.

- Use an old sheet or blanket to put things on and take them for a 'sledge' ride.

Note
He will want to discover his own limitations – so allow him to experiment without your help.

Suggested rhyme – Ride a cock-horse (page 193)

 # benefits

- Physical – Developing muscles, balance, flexibility and coordination.
- Other – Experimenting with weight and movement, and encouraging him to think.

# Follow the leader

## Instructions

Set up a daily exercise routine for yourself and encourage your toddler to watch and join in with you.

For example:

- Stretch your muscles as a warm up.
- Side bends, reaching your arms as high as possible while keeping your knees bent.
- Marching and clapping.
- Running on the spot.
- Star jumps/jumping jacks with arm movements.
- Skipping.

## Variations

- Try a daily aerobics session shown on television/video and let her watch you.
- Exercise with a friend and let her watch you.
- Start a daily exercise programme for the whole family.

## Precautions

- Don't push your toddler to do any particular exercise. Allow her to try to copy you in her own way.

- Remember to warm down.

Suggested rhyme – Slip one and two (page 195)

 **benefits**

- Physical – Developing movement skills, flexibility and coordination. Exercising many different muscles.
- Other – Learning by observation and learning good daily exercise habits.

# Wash the car

## Instructions

- Give your toddler a bowl or bucket of soapy water and a sponge and encourage him to help you wash the car.

- Let him experiment with washing other items such as his tricycle, toys, dolls, the fence and clothes.

- He may even choose to climb into the bucket and wash himself!

## Variations

- Encourage him to help you with household tasks such as washing windows and floors.

- Let him stand on a chair at the kitchen sink and wash plastic dishes and safe kitchen utensils, and wipe down the worktop.

## Precautions

- Supervise all water play. Children can drown in a small amount of water in a very short time.

- Do not let your child wash a car parked on the road.

Suggested rhyme – I hear thunder (page 187)

 # benefits

- Physical – Developing hand/eye coordination, hand skills, balance and flexibility.
- Other – Learning by imitating, and enjoying helping you. Learning new words.

# Little helper

## Instructions

- Encourage your toddler to be your 'little helper'.
- Ask him to fetch and carry things for you such as carrying the pegs out to the washing line and passing them to you one by one.
- Ask him to go to his room and get items for you like a nappy, his slippers, his boots, his hat.
- He can put his dirty clothes in the washing basket, get the dustpan and brush out of the cupboard and carry his plate out to the kitchen after meals.

## Variations

- Let him try bringing two or more items at once, or slightly heavier or more awkward items.
- Encourage him to help you to pick up and put away all his play things.

Note
Be patient. Sometimes having your toddler 'help you' means that it takes twice as long to get things done.

Suggested rhyme – Jack and Jill (page 189)

 # benefits

- Physical – Practising walking, balance, flexibility and coordination.
- Other – Developing a sense of achievement, learning by observation and linking objects, such as a brush and pan. Establishing routines. Learning new words.

# Finger painting

## Instructions

- Let your toddler paint with his fingers. (see recipes page 17)
- Cover the table or floor with some newspaper, so that he doesn't make a mess, then pour some finger paint onto a piece of wax paper or plastic.
- Show him how the paint can be swirled and moved around, using thumbs, fingers, hands and finger nails.
- Let him experiment with it.

## Variations

- Give him two or three different colours to mix and swirl together.
- Many different household substances can be used for finger painting.
- Ready-mixed children's paint can also be used.
- For outside play, mud makes very good finger paint.
- Encourage him to touch things with different textures such as the bark on trees, gravel, animals' fur, painted surfaces, crushed ice and so on.
- Add different textures to paint such as rice or sand.
- Mix cornflour with water until creamy, pour into dish and push fingers into it.

## Precaution

- Your toddler still enjoys tasting everything he touches, so be sure not to give him toxic substances to paint with.

Suggested rhyme – Tommy Thumb (page 199)

 # benefits

- **Physical – Developing hand skills and hand/eye coordination. Experiencing various textures.**
- **Other – Encouraging creativity and imagination, and time for relaxation. Learning new words.**

# Blowing

## Instructions

- Tie a fine ribbon to the end of a stick.
- Teach your toddler how to blow it to make it move.
- Blow the ribbon in his direction so that it flutters in his face.
- Have other children join in.

## Variations

- Collect a handful of dry leaves or petals and blow them, or watch the wind blowing them.
- Pick a blade of grass, flower, or dandelion clock to blow.
- Blow out candles.
- Float a cork on water to blow around.
- Blow a table tennis ball across a table.
- Show him how to put his mouth in the water with it closed and blow bubbles.

## Precautions

- Supervise water play. It takes very little time and water for a child to drown.
- Supervise burning candles.

Suggested rhyme – Jeremiah blow (page 189)

 # benefits

- Physical – Learning to control his breathing and exercise his lungs.
- Other – Learning about airflow and its effect on different objects. Learning by observing and experimenting.

Note
It takes time to learn how to do this. Give plenty of praise for trying.

# Sandcastles

## Instructions

- Take a bucket and spade on your next visit to the beach.
- Show your toddler how to make sandcastles.
- Collect shells and driftwood to decorate the sandcastles.
- She'll enjoy knocking them down each time you build them.
- Continue to encourage her to walk barefoot in the sand.

## Variations

- Dig a hole, put your feet in the hole and then let her shovel the sand back in to cover your feet. Then bury her feet.
- Give her items of different sizes and shapes to dig, fill, pour, sift, shovel and tip with.
- Let her play in a sand pit or dirt patch in the garden.
- Leaves, flowers, sticks, pine cones and other items can make play more interesting.

## Precautions

- The play area needs to be free of dangers, such as broken glass, dog mess, sharp objects.
- Cover the sand pit or dirt patch when not in use to keep dogs and cats out.
- Put on sunblock cream and a hat to prevent sunburn, and warm clothing on cold, windy days.

 # benefits

- Physical – Developing hand skills, hand/eye coordination, movement and flexibility.
- Other – Learning about size, shape, quantity and weight. Developing curiosity, imagination and vocabulary.

# Play ball

## Instructions

- Find a small lightweight ball that your toddler can easily hold in one hand.

- Put a large box or washing basket in front of him and show him how to throw the ball overarm forwards into the box.

- Let him practise doing this, praising him on every throw, whether it goes into the box or not.

## Variations

- Provide a pile of balls: rolled up tinfoil, socks, sponges, and pom-poms (see page 12), and have other children join in the game.

- Encourage him to throw with his left hand, right hand, overarm, underarm and both hands.

- Visit a pond and throw stones or pebbles into the water.

## Precautions

- Teach your toddler what he is and isn't allowed to throw, especially when playing inside.

- Supervise water play at all times. Toddlers can drown very quickly in a small amount of water.

Suggested rhyme – One two three a-leery (page 191)

 # benefits

- Physical – Developing balance, hand/eye coordination, flexibility and movement skills.
- Other – Learning ball-handling skills by watching others. Having fun and learning new words.

# Hockey

## Instructions

- Show your toddler how to hit a large lightweight ball around the house and garden using a kitchen roll tube, or rolled up newspaper.

- Then let her try to do it.

- Give her plenty of praise with every attempt.

- After a while find another lightweight bat and hit the ball to her, and then encourage her to hit or push it back to you.

## Variations

- Use a balloon, a dry bath sponge or some rolled up socks to replace the ball. The bat can be any kitchen utensil – like a wooden spoon, or a table tennis bat, or a plastic spade.

- Take your toddler to watch a hockey game.

 # benefits

- Physical – Developing hand/eye coordination, balance, movement skills and flexibility.
- Other – Learning through observation and exploring new capabilities. Learning new words.

Suggested rhyme – Sally go round (page 194)

# Playdough

## Instructions

- Clear a space on the worktop or table, or put some newspaper or a sheet of plastic on the floor for your toddler to use his playdough (see playdough recipes on page 14)

- Allow him to squeeze, poke, prod, roll, squash and manipulate his playdough.

- Provide some containers to put the playdough in, holes to push through, and blunt instruments to cut with.

## Variations

- Playdough can be enjoyed outside: sticking it on fences, walls and blocks of wood. He can decorate it with stones, leaves, sticks and flowers.

- He will want to experiment with the dough to see what it will do, like trying to bounce or roll it like a ball.

- You can buy plasticine.

## Precaution

- When buying plasticine make sure it is non-toxic.

Suggested rhymes – Half a pound of tuppenny rice (page 184)
Sing a song of sixpence (page 194)

 # benefits

- Physical – Developing hand/eye coordination and hand skills.

- Other – Experimenting with textures and shapes and developing creativity and imagination. Encouraging concentration. Learning new words.

# Music movement

## Instructions

- Sing action songs such as Incy wincy spider or Twinkle twinkle.
- Use homemade instruments to make sounds to the rhythm of your song. (See page 13)
- If you play a musical instrument, play the tune and sing along or stamp your foot to the beat.

## Variations

- Make up your own songs and rhythms.
- March, dance, sing and play instruments together with music on the radio. (Anything that makes a noise is a musical instrument).
- Provide her with plenty of opportunities to watch other people doing different types of dancing.

## Precaution

- Let her experiment with movement to music with plenty of praise – laughing at her may cause her to lose confidence.

 # benefits

- Physical – Improving balance, flexibility, movement skills and coordination.
- Other – Developing a sense of rhythm, and learning through observation. Learning to rhyme.

# Bubble fun

## Instructions

- Make up some bubbles in a bowl. (see page 18 for recipes)
- Make a loop with a pipe cleaner or wire coat hanger, or find a toy or utensil with a hole in that will make a good bubble blower.
- Blow bubbles and let them float around the room for your toddler or chase, poke, clap or stamp.

## Variations

- Have other children join in blowing and chasing the bubbles.
- Play this outside and watch the bubbles blow around in the breeze.
- Make paper planes and fly them around the room for her to chase and catch.

## Precautions

- If you buy bubbles check they carry the CE mark.
- Clean up spillages so that no one slips over in the soap.

Suggested rhyme – Old King Cole (page 190)

# benefits

- Physical – Developing balance, hand/eye coordination, movement skills and flexibility.
- Other – Having fun, experimenting and learning by observation. Learning new words and socialising.

# Farm animals

## Instructions

- Take your toddler to visit a farm.
- Show him each of the farm animals that he's learnt about in his books and from pictures and count them.
- Give him time to sit and watch what each animal does.
- Show him how to imitate the animals' movements and sounds.

## Variations

- Visit a lake with ducks, geese, swans and other birds and let him feed them some bread.
- Visit a pet shop and wander around quietly together looking at the animals, naming them, talking about them and counting how many there are.
- Visit friends who have pets, or get a pet of your own.
- Sing animal songs like Old MacDonald.

## Precautions

- Try to avoid frightening experiences with animals that may cause him to lose his confidence.
- Only visit farms which are open to the public.

- Telephone first and ask for information on opening times and hygiene details.

- Do not encourage children to touch animals, their enclosures or droppings. Wash and dry hands immediately if they do so or carry anti-bacterial wipes to use if facilities are not available nearby.

- On leaving animal enclosure wash hands with soap and warm, running water. Dry with paper towels.

- Do not eat when walking around the animals. Only eat in cafe or picnic areas – away from the animals – and always wash and dry hands before eating.

- Tell children not to put their fingers in their mouths and supervise children closely around animals.

- Thoroughly clean shoes after farm visit – separate footwear such as boots would be good. Wash and dry hands thoroughly after cleaning shoes.

- Pregnant women should avoid sheep at lambing time.

- Seek medical advice if your toddler has diarrhoea and/or vomiting after farm visit.

- Farm visits should be fun for children, but adults must be aware of health risks such as E coli 0157 or infections in the farm environment, and of sensible precautions to reduce these risks.

# benefits

- **Physical – Exercise and fresh air.**
- **Other – Observing movement and curiosity.**

# Run run!

## Instructions

- Run with your toddler from one side of the room to the other and back again.
- Have other children join in and encourage them to run back and forth.
- Clap and give praise each time they reach the wall.

## Variations

- Put an obstacle in the middle of the room like a tunnel made with a blanket, or a cushion to climb over so that they stop, tackle the obstacle, and then run to the end.
- Find open spaces to run in: the back garden, a park, a farm, the beach.
- Have races and let her win most of the time.
- Take her to watch athletics at the park.

## Precautions

- Make sure her movement isn't limited by restrictive clothing.
- After energetic play offer her a drink of water, and make sure she doesn't get cold.

Suggested rhyme – To market, to market (page 199)

 # benefits

- Physical – Developing balance, movement skills, flexibility and coordination.
- Other – Learning to observe, interact with and think about others.

# Kick the ball

## Instructions

- Use a lightweight ball that is large enough for your toddler to kick easily (at least 13 cm/5 inches diameter).

- Put the ball on the floor and kick it back and forth against a wall or between two of you so that your toddler can watch.

- Then kick the ball slowly towards him and encourage him to kick it back.

- Repeat this, with plenty of praise for trying, until he has had enough.

## Variations

- Try kicking a balloon, a ball made of tinfoil, a piece of polystyrene, a dry bath sponge, a beach ball, or a pile of dry leaves or grass clippings in the garden.

- Take your toddler to watch children playing football.

## Precautions

- Give plenty of praise with each attempt at kicking, even when he misses.

- Don't expect him to kick a ball that is too small, too large or too heavy.

 # benefits

- Physical – Developing balance, coordination, movement skills and flexibility.
- Other – Learning through observation and exploring new capabilities. Learning new words.

# Climbing

## Instructions

- Let your toddler climb up and down the stairs or on and off the couch.
- Teach her how to climb down backwards safely.

## Variations

- Encourage her to climb in and out of the car by herself when you go places.
- Let her practise climbing on and off the bed.
- Take her to a playground with safe climbing equipment appropriate for her size.

## Precautions

- Supervise all climbing activities.
- Make sure the climbing apparatus is sturdy and won't tip over.
- Check that she can't reach objects that you don't want her to have and keep car doors closed so that she doesn't play in the car alone.
- Make sure that she can't climb up to a window that she may fall out of.
- Use child-locks on the car and only allow her to climb out on the pavement side.

Suggested rhyme – Grand old Duke of York (page 184)

 # benefits

- Physical – Developing balance, flexibility, coordination and movement skills.
- Other – Exploring new capabilities and independence. Learning through observation. Learning new words.

# Got you

## Instructions

- Play tig with your toddler around the back garden, chasing him at his own pace, and then when you catch him, say 'Got you!'

- Have other children join in too, so that he sees you chase and catch them.

- Once he understands the game let him chase you (running at his pace) and catch you, both saying 'Got you!'

## Variations

- Have races running side by side holding hands.

- Let him try to catch you as you run in a circle around an obstacle, and change direction several times, letting him catch you often. Then change places and you try to catch him.

## Precautions

- Make sure his movement isn't limited by restrictive clothing.

- After energetic play offer him a drink of water, and make sure he doesn't get cold.

Suggested rhyme – One little baby rocking in a tree (page 190)

# benefits

- Physical – Developing balance and movement skills.
- Other – Learning by observation, and beginning to interact and think about others. Having fun.

# section **3**

## 2–2 ½ years

**Bookbug says:**

Books don't have to stay on the bookshelf. Keep books in toy boxes or on low shelves so your toddler can play with them.

# Gentle touch

## Instructions

- In the evening before bedtime, begin to relax your toddler with quiet games, or reading.

- Sit with her and stroke her back, arms, legs, and massage her hands and fingers, feet and toes.

- Once she's in bed, finish the massage with a gentle back rub and several long, light, loving strokes from head to foot.

## Variations

- Use massage strokes to soothe your toddler when she's ill, over-excited or angry.

- Get to know what massage she likes the most.

- If she has a favourite cloth or blanket that she likes the feel of, wrap it around your hand for massaging, or wrap her snugly in her blanket.

- If you have a pet, teach her how to stroke and pat it lovingly and gently, and point out the animal's response to her.

- Let her see you massaging other members of the family.

## Precautions

- If you or your toddler are not enjoying this activity, stop and try again another day.

- Some children may become excitable if the touch is too gentle.

Suggested rhyme – I love little kitty (page 188)

# benefits

- **Physical – Developing loving touch and body awareness. Encouraging relaxation.**
- **Other – Enhancing parent/child relationships and learning stress management.**

# Wash hands

## Instructions

- Teach your toddler how to wash and dry her hands.
- Have a little step handy so she can reach into the basin.
- Turn the cold water on and off for her and pass her the soap.
- Make handwashing a habit before and after meals and after using the toilet.

## Variations

- Let her try to clean her own teeth after each meal with some help from you.
- Encourage her to brush or comb her hair and to feed herself with a spoon and fork.

## Precaution

- Supervise your toddler in the bathroom at all times.

Note
It takes toddlers twice as long as an adult to do these activities.
Be patient and let her learn and practise new skills.

 # benefits

- Physical – Developing hand skills, coordination and balance.
- Other – Asserting independence and a sense of achievement by attempting activities she has learnt by watching others. Establishing healthy routines.

# Let's draw

## Instructions

- Let your toddler draw with a chunky crayon while you watch him.
- Let him draw in any way he wants.
- Let him hold the crayon in his own way and use whichever hand he chooses.
- Give plenty of praise for all his efforts.

## Variations

- Show him how to draw in wet sand with a stick.
- Give him paint (see recipes page 17), a thick brush and large pieces of paper to paint on. Use two or three primary colours and tell him the names of the colours.
- Flour can be scattered on the table lightly and shapes drawn in it with fingers.

## Precautions

- Pencils and paint brushes can be very sharp – always supervise your toddler when he is using them.
- Make sure he is not putting things in his mouth that are dangerous or poisonous.

Suggested rhyme – Roses are red (page 194)

 # benefits

- Physical – Developing hand skills and hand/eye coordination.
- Other – Encouraging him to think and use his imagination. Learning by observation. Learning new words.

# Stick and paste

## Instructions

- Provide a large sheet of paper or cardboard to glue things on.
- Glue can be homemade (see recipes page 16) or bought: a glue stick or PVA glue watered down.
- Collect a variety of items for your toddler to glue or paste with, such as scraps of material, paper, junk mail, leaves, straws, string, wool, shells and sweet wrappers.

## Variations

- Help her decorate egg boxes or boxes to keep things in.
- Glue together kitchen junk such as cereal boxes, egg boxes, and kitchen roll tubes to make a 3-D model.
- Collect a few magnets and show her how to attach things to the fridge with them: pictures, ribbons and scraps of material.
- Continue to encourage play with building blocks. (see page 44)
- She will enjoy single-shape puzzles where each piece is one thing (like a car or a duck) and has a little handle.

## Precaution

- Wear old clothes or an apron when playing with glue.

 # benefits

- Physical – Developing hand/eye coordination and hand skills.
- Other – Learning by watching and copying others. Encouraging creativity and imagination.

# Road works

## Instructions

- Turn the sand pit into a major construction area.

- Provide containers for digging and pouring, like plastic cups, boxes, tubs, bottles and spoons.

- Provide equipment for bridges, roads and tunnels, such as cardboard tubes, pieces of cardboard, blocks of wood.

- Trucks, cars and bulldozers can be made from blocks of wood or cardboard boxes.

- Sink a bowl in the sand filled with water to make a lake and float things on it.

- Your toddler and other children will spend many hours playing, digging, constructing and experimenting in the sand pit.

- Join in the games with him sometimes.

## Variations

- If you can't have a sand pit, mark off a patch of garden for the children to use.

- Visit a beach or sandy river and take containers with you, for your toddler to experiment with in the sand.

- Help your toddler set up an area on the floor inside with roads, bridges, tunnels and vehicles using blocks, cardboard, paper, boxes and other household items.

## Precautions

- Cover the sand pit when not in use to keep dogs and cats out.
- Put on sunblock cream and a hat to prevent sunburn and warm clothing on cold, windy days.

Suggested rhyme – The wheels on the bus (page 198)

# benefits

- **Physical – Developing hand skills and coordination. Exercising many different muscles.**
- **Other – Discovering the concepts of size, shape, quantity and weight. Learning to observe and interact with others. Learning new words.**

# Cooking fun

## Instructions

- Have your toddler help you with the baking: stirring, mixing and kneading.
- Provide him with a space on the worktop or table and a bowl of mixture and let him copy what you're doing.
- Make and name simple shapes – square, triangle, circle.
- Put their 'creations' in the oven with yours for baking.

## Variations

- Give him playdough (see recipes page 14), clay or pastry. You can even make his own stove and oven from a large cardboard box.
- Give him utensils such as a rolling pin, baking trays, biscuit cutters and blunt cutting utensils to use. Use a fork for patterns.
- Begin counting lessons by counting the number of dough shapes he has made.

## Precautions

- Do not leave your toddler in the kitchen alone.
- Teach him the difference between hot and cold.
- Turn saucepan handles inwards so they are not over the edges of the cooker, or use a cooker guard.

Suggested rhymes –  Pat-a-cake (page 191)
Hot cross buns (page 185)

 # benefits

- Physical – Developing hand and movement skills, hand/eye coordination and learning to concentrate.
- Other – Learning through observation and learning new words. Encouraging creativity and imagination.

# Stepping

## Instructions

- Lie a ladder down on the grass for your toddler to play with.

- Have him step between the rungs of the ladder from one end to the other.

- Then ask him to turn around and step on each rung as he walks back. To do this you will need to hold his hand for balance or he can bend over and walk on his hands and feet like a crab.

- Ask him to walk along with one foot either side of the ladder.

## Variations

- Encourage him to move sideways along the ladder, feet at one side, hands at the other.

- Cut out some large stepping stones from newspaper, place them on the floor in a line fairly close together and try the same activities as above.

- On rainy days put on boots and step in puddles. Also step carefully between puddles and then run together trying to dodge the puddles.

- When walking along the footpath play a game where you're not allowed to stand on any cracks.

- Have other children join in.

Note
If he becomes frustrated and has difficulty with the game leave it and let him go back to it when he's ready.

Suggested rhymes – Two little feet (page 200)

 # benefits

- **Physical – Balancing on one foot, foot/eye coordination, movement skills and coordination.**
- **Other – Learning by observing and imitating.**

# Singing

## Instructions

- Sing – Hickory Dickory Dock
  The mouse ran up the clock,
  The clock struck one,
  The mouse ran down,
  Hickory Dickory Dock.

- Teach your toddler how to do the hand actions of a mouse running up a clock by walking his fingers up the wall as far as he can reach.

- Then with the other hand point a finger in the air to signal the 'clock struck one', and then walk the mouse down the wall again.

- Repeat this quickly and then slowly – start slowly as they learn the song, then quicken the pace.

## Variation

- Make up your own songs and put actions to them.

See the section at the back of this book and the play@home Baby Book for further action songs and rhymes.

Note
Your toddler may not learn all the words of a song, but will join in on his favourite chorus or phrases.
Suggested rhymes – Incy wincy spider (page 188)
Wiggle your fingers (page 201)

# benefits

- **Physical – Improving hand/eye and upper body coordination. Coordinating movement with words.**
- **Other – Developing a sense of rhythm, and learning through observation, learning to associate words with actions.**

# Tumbling tots

### Instructions

- Teach your toddler how to do a forward roll:
  1. Have him bend over and put his hands on the carpet close to his feet, and look at you between his legs so that his chin is on his chest.
  2. Support the back of his head and neck with one hand so that he keeps his chin on his chest.
  3. With the other hand gently roll him over until he is lying on his back on the floor.
  4. Repeat if enjoyed by your child.

### Variations

- Rolling: Lying him on his tummy, roll him over and over on the floor and then back the other way. Then encourage him to try it himself.

- Try these activities outside on the grass, or down a slight slope.

### Precautions

- Make sure his chin is tucked into his chest when rolling to prevent neck injury.

- Practise these activities on a soft surface to avoid injury.

- Don't force him with these activities, because he may lose confidence.
- For children with additional needs, please seek the advice of your therapist before attempting this activity.

Suggested rhyme – Ten in the bed (page 196)

# benefits

- **Physical – Developing balance, movement skills and coordination.**
- **Other – Developing new skills and learning by observation.**

# Parachutes

## Instructions

- Find a large scarf or light piece of fabric.
- Hold two corners of the scarf and encourage your toddler to hold the other corners.
- Together, flap the scarf up in the air so that when you bring it down it catches some wind and puffs up.
- Flap it up and down, encouraging him to lift it as high as he can and then bring his arms down as low as he can.

## Variations

- Blow up a balloon and rest it on the scarf, so that when you lift the scarf up the balloon becomes airborne. Encourage him to catch the balloon. Repeat this several times.
- Try putting other light items on the scarf like dried leaves or a soft toy.
- Play this game while you chant or sing, or play some music to move to.

## Precaution

- Find a safe area with plenty of space to play this game.

Suggested rhymes – Peter rabbit (page 192)
Two little dicky birds (page 200)

 # benefits

- Physical – Developing movement skills, balance and coordination.
- Other – Learning about weight and learning new words.

# Aeroplanes

## Instructions

- Encourage your toddler and his friends to be aeroplanes: running around outside with their arms stretched out like wings, making aeroplane sounds.

- Have them land their planes to pick up and drop off passengers.

- Make some 'stop' and 'go' signs (red and green) and encourage them to obey when you hold them up.

## Variations

- Let them pretend to be birds, gliders, helicopters or bumble bees.

- Take them to visit an airport, or to watch hang-gliders, or to see the seagulls on a windy day at the beach.

Note
Your toddler might like to make up his own game rather than take part in any structured play. Let him do this.

Suggested rhyme – Five little monkeys (page 183)

 # benefits

- **Physical – Developing balance, coordination and movement skills.**
- **Other – Learning by observing, interacting with and thinking about others. Introducing road safety.**

# Animal visit

## Instructions

- Take your toddler to visit a zoo, park, farm or aquarium.
- See if he can name the animals he recognises from the books and pictures you've shown him.
- Give him plenty of time to stop and watch the animals that interest him, especially their movement.
- Time the visit so that he can see some animals being fed.
- Count how many animals he can see.
- Encourage him to copy the animals' movements and sounds.

## Variations

- Show him pictures and tell stories about the particular animals before you go to see them.
- Show him nature and pet programmes. Visit friends who have pets.
- Sing animal songs such as 'Mamma's taking us to the zoo tomorrow', 'Old MacDonald had a farm' or 'Five little ducks'.

## Precautions

- Seeing too many animals all in one day can be tiring.
- Always wash hands with anti-bacterial soap in running clean water after touching animals.
- Always clean shoes thoroughly after visits to animals outdoors.

(See page 95 for further precautions when visiting animals.)

# benefits

- **Physical – Outings with exercise and fresh air. Learning movement skills.**
- **Other – Observing and imitating movement and behaviour learning new words. Learning to count.**

# Jumping beans

## Instructions

- Put an old cushion or mattress on the floor for your toddler and friends to jump on.
- Let him experiment with jumping on the floor and then jumping on the cushion.
- Hold hands and jump together, or form a circle with other children and jump around.

## Variations

- Put on the radio, chant rhymes, or sing songs and jump around the room together to the beat.
- Play musical bumps.
- Jump off a low step yourself and then encourage him to jump while holding your hand.
- Jump in puddles and on shadows.

## Precaution

- Teach him to land on his feet with his knees slightly bent, so that he learns the correct way to prevent injury.

Suggested rhyme – Three tiny kittens (page 199)

 **benefits**

- Physical – Developing coordination and balance.
- Other – Learning by observing and imitating others. Experiencing different surfaces when landing.

# Bouncing ball

## Instructions

- Show your toddler how to drop a ball to the ground, let it bounce and catch it in two hands.
- Then let the ball bounce away from you until it stops.
- Give your toddler the opportunity to experiment with dropping and throwing the ball and chasing it as it bounces.

## Variations

- Let him stand at the top of a few steps, drop it down the steps, retrieve it and do it again and again.
- Let him bounce it on different surfaces such as grass, sand, concrete, carpet and try to bounce it in water.
- Find a long pipe or tube (or join several tubes together) so that he can drop the ball in at one end and watch it bounce out the other end.
- Enable him to watch older children playing with a ball and watch sports such as volleyball, netball and basketball.

## Precaution

- Make sure the play area is fenced so that your toddler cannot chase a ball onto the road.

Suggested rhyme – One potato, two potato (page 191)

Note
Don't expect him to catch the ball in the air yet.

# benefits

- **Physical – Developing ball skills, balance and coordination.**
- **Other – Learning by observation.**

# Obstacle course

## Instructions

- Set up a course in the garden for your toddler to crawl through tunnels, step over obstacles, climb up and down and under and over. (Use boxes, wood, ropes for crawling under and so on).

- Get down on the ground and show him how to do it.

- Let him do it a few times and then have a race and let him win.

- Include other children in this game.

## Variations

- Set up a course inside with upside down chairs, boxes, blankets, cushions, tables and so on.

- Provide the opportunity for him to play in an adventure playground with plenty of supervision and to watch other children.

## Precaution

- If he's likely to fall ensure he will fall on carpet, or something soft.

Suggested rhyme – Jack be nimble (page 189)

 # benefits

- Physical – Developing balance, coordination.
- Other – Learning through observing, imitating and interacting with others. Learning new words.

# Monkey swing

## Instructions

- Hold a broom handle parallel to the ground between two adults.

- Encourage your toddler to hold onto it, swing on it, and lift his feet up off the ground.

- When he has had a rest, have him hold onto the broom handle again and then lift him up so that his feet are just a few centimetres off the ground. Repeat this several times.

## Variations

- Encourage him to swing on bars in a children's playground.

- Enrol him in a toddler movement class.

- Give him the opportunity to watch monkeys swinging at the zoo.

## Precaution

- Let your toddler discover his own limitation, so that he doesn't lose confidence in attempting this activity.

Suggested rhyme – Five little monkeys (page 183)

 # benefits

- Physical – Developing upper body strength.
- Other – Learning through observation. Learning new skills.

# section **4**

2 ½–3 years

**Bookbug says:**

Sharing books together will inspire your child to begin drawing, writing and making up their own stories.

# Sleepy cats

## Instructions

- Lie beside your child. Let her pretend to be a cat and stretch out her arms and legs, then stroke her as she lies quietly.

- Make up a story about a cat stretching out in the sunshine or lying in front of the fire.

- While you tell the story, use a natural massage oil (see page 171) to slowly and gently massage down her back, arms and legs.

- Finish with a cuddle.

## Variations

- Read her favourite books as you sit together quietly.

- Have a bath together and encourage her to lie back and float in the water, with you supporting her body.

- Try these activities before bedtime, or if she's unwell or agitated.

## Precautions

- Some toddlers are extremely active and won't sit still for long.

- Avoid activities in the water that may cause her to lose her confidence.

Suggested rhyme – Pussy cat pussy cat (page 193)

 # benefits

- Physical – Promoting general body control through relaxation.
- Other – Increasing body awareness and an enhanced parent/child relationship.

# Draw and dress

## Instructions

- Lie your child down on a big piece of paper and draw around her.

- Give your child a selection of her clothes varying from underwear to outdoor clothing.

- Encourage her to put the clothing on the outline.

- Allow her to make mistakes.

- Talk about what she is doing.

## Variations

- Repeat the activity with her dressing your outline.

- Use dressing-up clothes, beads, bangles, hats, scarves, slippers, shoes to dress herself and you.

- Let her dress up her teddy and dolls.

- Try musical dressing up; when the music stops put on a piece of clothing.

- Play Simon says – 'put on a hat', 'put on a sock' or in the bath 'wash your tummy'.

- Try face painting.

- Practise brushing hair, brushing teeth, washing face.

- Put out the clothing for your child to select, avoiding difficult fastenings and awkward clothing. Try and select easy-opening and elasticated-waist garments, such as sweatshirts, T-shirts, leggings, joggers.

Note
Have a mirror available so that she can see herself.

Allow your child to make mistakes when she is learning to dress herself.
Only correct her when necessary, for example, if shoes are on the wrong feet.

Suggested rhyme – Hush-a-bye baby (page 186)

# benefits

- Physical – General coordination.
- Other – Having fun, learning about herself and how to dress through play. Asserting independence. Encouraging language development.

# Kitchen magic

## Instructions

- Encourage your toddler to help you in the kitchen with food preparation.

- Let her open a packet of whipped pudding. Help her measure milk and pour into a large bowl. Let her spoon packet mix into the bowl and help her whisk the mixture so that she can see how it 'magically' changes.

- Once set, let her decorate with sugar strands.

## Variations

- Provide her with the opportunity to see how a solid ice cube melts, how sugar dissolves in water and how baking soda froths when stirred into warm milk.

- Let her get the fruit and vegetables and wash them for you. Talk about their different sizes and shapes.

- While baking, let her use some dough to make her own creation. Cook this along with yours.

## Precautions

- Supervise your toddler at all times in the kitchen. Reinforce the danger of the hot cooker to her.

- Make sure she can't burn herself with the hot tap.

- Turn saucepan handles inwards so they are not over the edges of the cooker, or use a cooker guard.

Suggested rhymes – The doughnut song (page 197)
Five currant buns (page 182)

# benefits

- **Physical – Learning hand skills and hand/eye coordination.**
- **Other – Learning by observation and learning new words. Discovering the concepts of measures and weights and observing change.**

# Bowling

## Instructions

- Stand five or six empty plastic bottles together, in a bunch, on the floor.

- Show your toddler how to roll a large, light ball along the floor to knock all the bottles over.

- Count how many bottles have been knocked over.

- Stand the bottles up again, have her stand 2 metres away from them and roll the ball towards them. Repeat several times.

- Give plenty of praise, with every attempt.

## Variations

- Place two obstacles on the ground, 1 metre apart, and have her roll the ball between them; roll it back again.

- Roll a ball into a box.

- Have other children play, encouraging them to take turns.

- Pour a little sand in the bottles to make them more stable.

## Precaution

- Don't use plastic bottles that have contained poisonous or harmful substances in case she tries to drink from them.

Suggested rhyme – Ten green bottles (page 195)

 # benefits

- Physical – Learning ball skills and developing balance and coordination.
- Other – Having fun, and learning to interact and think about others. Learning to count.

# Gardening

## Instructions

- Show your toddler how vegetables and flowers grow.

- Let her have her own garden plot, spade and trowel.

- Plant some of her favourite vegetables or those that are easy to grow and are tasty.

- Interesting vegetables to grow are carrots, beans, radishes and tomatoes.

- Tend them together, watch their progress and discuss the insects that eat them.

- Pick the produce together and include it in your meals.

## Variations

- Grow a flower garden with many different colours, varieties and smells. Discuss the bees, butterflies and other insects that are found in the flowerbed.

- Pick flowers together to arrange in a vase or to give to someone.

- Grow plants in pots or plastic containers both inside and outside.

- Try growing bean sprouts together, or growing seeds on a piece of damp cloth, or sprouting a carrot.

## Precautions

- Provide her with tools that are the right size for her.

- Toddlers imitate everything you do so she may pull out a whole lot of plants calling them weeds, and she may pick a whole crop of green tomatoes for you thinking that she's being helpful.

- Remember some plants are harmful, supervise your toddler.

Suggested rhymes – I had a little cherry stone (page 186)
I have a little garden (page 187)

# benefits

- **Physical – Developing hand skills, hand/eye coordination.**
- **Other – Learning about nature and how plants grow. Learning by observation and learning new words.**

# Hokey cokey

## Instructions

- Sing this song and do the actions, encouraging your toddler to imitate you. (Have others join in too). To do the Hokey cokey wriggle your body from side to side.

You put your right hand in
Your put your right hand out
You put your right hand in
And you shake it all about
You do the 'hokey cokey' and
You turn around

That's what it's all about – see!
Repeat verses using 'left hand',
'right foot', 'left foot',
'right ear','left ear' and finally
'whole self'!

## Variations

- Sing this song:

## Dingle Dangle Scarecrow

When all the cows were sleeping
And the sun had gone to bed
Up jumped the scarecrow

And this is what he said:
I'm a Dingle Dangle Scarecrow
With a flippy, floppy hat
I can shake my hands like this
And shake my feet like that
When all the hens were roosting
And the moon behind the cloud
Up jumped the scarecrow
And shouted very loud...

- Try other action songs. Make up your own.
- Action tapes and videos can be borrowed from your library for a small fee.

## Precaution

- Don't force your toddler to join in. Let her take her time and watch others playing.

# benefits

- **Physical – Developing balance, coordination, flexibility and movement skills. Teaches body awareness.**
- **Other – Having fun and learning to interact and think about others. Learning by observation and learning new words.**

# Tall and small

## Instructions

- Teach your toddler how to be tall: take a big breath in, push out your chest and stand as tall as you can.

- Then become small: blow out your breath, round your shoulders and crouch down.

- Repeat this again a few times and then do the same activity while walking around the room: walk tall on tiptoes and be small on knees.

## Variations

- Pretend to be a balloon: breathe in as you blow up the balloon and become as large and round as you can and then scrunch up into a ball as you blow your breath out. Repeat this several times.

- Be a daisy: breathe in and spread your arms like petals in the sunshine and then breathe out, wrap your arms around you and crouch down, to go to sleep. Repeat.

Suggested rhyme – I'm a little teapot (page 188)

 # benefits

- Physical – Stretching and coordinating breathing with movements.
- Other – Using her imagination and learning to wind down. Learning new words.

# Board walk

## Instructions

- Place a ladder or board on a slight slope and help your toddler move up and down it.
- Have her try this sitting on her bottom, pushing herself up with her hands and feet.
- She can climb up forwards on hands and feet, or walk up while holding your hand.

## Variations

- Help her to balance and move along a low wall.
- Include boards or ladders in an obstacle course outside. (see page 134)
- Take her for a walk past a building site where she can watch builders climbing up and down ladders.

## Precautions

- The safest way to prevent climbing accidents is to teach her how to climb both up and down.
- Toddlers have no sense of danger. Supervise all climbing activities.

 # benefits

- Physical – Developing balance and coordination.
- Other – Finding out about height and by observation.

# Row the boat

## Instructions

- Sit on the floor with your legs straddled and your toddler sitting between your legs with her back to you. Have her hold your hands and then pretend to row the boat, rocking back and forth together.

  Sing Row, row, row your boat
  Gently down the stream,
  Merrily, merrily, merrily, merrily,
  Life is but a dream.
- Repeat this quickly and then slowly.
- Add some music.

## Variations

- See-saw: sit facing each other in the straddle position holding hands. Rock back and forth singing or chanting a rhyme.

- Lie back on your elbows with knees bent and feet to feet. (Your left foot flat against her right foot, and your right foot flat against her left). Push each foot back and forth, like riding a bicycle. Gradually increase the resistance so that she has to push harder against your feet.

 # benefits

- Physical – Developing coordination and rhythm.
- Other – Having fun and learning to interact and to think about others. Learning rhythm.

# Up to the top

## Instructions

- Find a steep hill and climb up to the top with your toddler to see what can be seen from there. Run or roll back down again.

- Climb up the steps to the top of a chute and slide down the other side.

- Find an easy gate to climb and teach her how to climb up and over it and down the other side.

## Variations

- Visit a children's playground where there is a variety of equipment to climb on.

- Take walks together where the tracks are moderately steep and/or include steps.

- In department stores take the stairs, escalators and lifts and play counting games as you go up and down.

- Set up your own obstacle course at home (see page 134).

- Join a toddler movement class.

## Precautions

- Supervise all climbing activities – toddlers have no sense of danger. The safest way to minimise climbing accidents is to teach them how to climb both up and down first.

- Ensure the height of the equipment they're climbing and the surface underneath it is safe.

Note
Ask at your local library or tourist information office for information on local walks.

Suggested rhyme – Grand old Duke of York (page 184)

 **benefits**

- **Physical – Developing movement skills, balance and coordination.**
- **Other – Enjoying exercise and movement with you as role model. Encouraging exploring and curiosity.**

# Horse play

## Instructions

- Make your toddler a stick horse: stuff a paper bag with newspaper and draw eyes and ears on it for the horse's head, a ribbon for reins, and attach it to a broom handle.

- Show her how to ride around the garden on it making horse sounds and chanting rhymes.

  Ride a cock-horse
  To Banbury Cross,
  To see a fine lady,
  Upon a white horse.
  With rings on her fingers
  And bells on her toes,
  She shall have music
  Wherever she goes.

## Variations

- Make up your own rhymes and songs to trot to and include music.

- Sit her astride your knee and sing to the tune of the Mulberry Bush song 'This is the way we ride a horse'.

- Find a long piece of rope that can be a horse and have other children all hop on and ride it around the garden together.

- Change the speed and direction several times.

## Precautions

- Toddlers enjoy swinging things in the air, so put the horses away when they've finished riding them, to avoid injuries.

- Supervise this activity.

- After this activity offer her a drink of water and ensure she cools down slowly.

 # benefits

- **Physical – Developing balance, flexibility, lower body coordination and movement skills.**
- **Other – Using her imagination, developing rhythm and learning by observation.**

# Up and over

## Instructions

- Use a lightweight, soft ball that your toddler can easily hold in one hand.

- Set up two chairs facing back to back with a piece of string tied between them.

- Using an overarm throw, show her how to throw the ball over the string in an upward arc.

- She can then run to the other side and try to throw it back again.

## Variations

- Vary the height of the string.

- Replace the ball with a bean bag (see page 13), a ball made of aluminium foil, or a wet sponge can be fun on a hot day.

- Throw the ball over a bush, wall, wheelbarrow or other object.

- Let her stand or sit on a step to throw the ball.

- Have playmates join in and encourage them to take turns at throwing.

- This can be adapted to indoor play for rainy days using soft items to throw such as a ball of wool, a soft toy or socks.

## Precautions

- Your toddler may lose confidence if she gets hit by a ball, so don't expect her to catch the ball in the air.

- Avoid conflict by ensuring she knows what she is and is not allowed to throw around.

# benefits

- Physical – Developing balance, coordination and movement skills.

- Other – Learning ball skills and observation. Experimenting with weight and gravity and learning to count.

# Truck driver

## Instructions

- Encourage your toddler to pretend to be a truck driver.

- Set up a road around the house and garden using foot paths, grass, tight corners, trees for roundabouts, boxes for tunnels and so on.

- Have your toddler walk around the course, making the sound of a truck and pretending to use the steering wheel. (A paper plate or lid can be used as a steering wheel).

- When she has done it a few times, have her turn and go in the opposite direction around the course.

- Then ask her to drive very fast and run around the course.

## Variations

- Let her pretend to be a motorbike, car, tractor or bus.

- Make believe a petrol station, shop, bus stop and traffic lights where she stops for various reasons.

- She could ride a sit-on toy, tricycle or horse (see page 160) around the course.

## Precautions

- Toddlers see things differently from adults so give her the opportunity to adapt things to suit her own play.

- Ensure all garden fences and gates are secure so that she does not come to any harm.

Suggested rhyme – Horsey horsey (page 185)
Down at the station (page 181)

 **benefits**

- **Physical – Developing balance, coordination and movement skills.**

- **Other – Beginning to develop imagination and following directions.**

# Frog hop

## Instructions

- Tell a story about a frog to your toddler and show her a picture of one.
- You may even find one for her if you visit a country park.
- Show her how to frog hop around the garden, make noises like frogs and flick out her tongue to catch flies.
- Have other children join in frog hopping.
- Provide obstacles to frog hop over.
- Teach her how to land on both feet with her knees bent.

## Variations

- Play the same game pretending to be a grasshopper, cricket or sparrow.
- Cut out stepping stones from a piece of newspaper and encourage her to jump from one stone to another.
- Encourage her to jump from various heights (no higher than her waist) onto a soft surface, landing with her knees slightly bent.

## Precaution

- Do not force her to jump from a height if she does not want to as this may cause her to lose confidence.

Suggested rhyme – Three little speckled frogs (page 198)

 # benefits

- Physical – Developing balance and movement skills.
- Other – Learning to observe, learning by example.

# Swan lake

### Instructions

- Find some classical music on the radio and glide around the lounge like a ballet dancer.
- Encourage your toddler to imitate your gliding, swaying, bending and arm movements.
- Allow her to develop her own style of dancing to music.

### Variations

- Put on fast and slow music and move to the beat together.
- Do a dance with her standing on your feet and moving with you.
- Try country and western music and Scottish country dance music, tap your feet and lock arms and dance around in a circle to music.
- Give her the opportunity to watch others dancing and enjoying music.

### Precaution

- Don't laugh at your toddler's attempt to dance as she may become self-conscious about dancing.

Suggested rhyme – Dance to your daddy (page 181)

 # benefits

- Physical – Improving balance, coordination and movement skills.
- Other – Developing a sense of rhythm, learning by observation and having fun. Encouraging creativity and imagination.

# Toddler massage

- Provide your toddler with plenty of cuddles, loving touch and close contact every day.

- Make the most of opportunities to massage him when he's sitting quietly looking at books or toys, during bath time, while you're dressing him, at bedtime or any other time he needs calming or settling.

- Use cuddles and reassuring touch to dispel your toddler's anxieties and fears and to help both of you to deal with frustration and tantrums.

- Allow him to give permission to be massaged or cuddled and to break contact when he chooses.

- Be aware of your toddler's likes and dislikes with loving touch and adapt your massage technique accordingly.

- All toddlers, including those with additional needs, respond well to cuddles and loving touch.

- The following pages appear in the play@home Baby Book. The strokes can be used on your toddlers too, so we have copied them here for you to follow.

# Massage techniques

## Instructions

- Make sure your shoulders and hands are relaxed and make your movements slow and rhythmical, maintaining continuous skin contact as much as possible.

- Choose a comfortable position for yourself to massage your toddler, making sure that you are not twisting or straining your back.

There are two main techniques used:

- Stroking – gliding gently along the surface of the skin.

- Kneading – gently moving the muscles underneath the skin.

- Repeat each technique 2–3 times, less for the face, which is a sensitive area.

- Be flexible, do more of the strokes that your toddler obviously likes.

- Massage oils: use natural oils because what is put on your toddler's skin may be absorbed into the body. Your chemist or health shop will advise you on what is available. Warm the oil by rubbing it on your hands first.

# The front of the body

Begin with the front so that you can establish eye contact and talk to your toddler.

## The legs

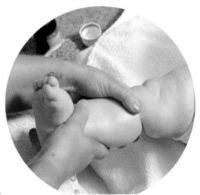

- Stroke from top of thighs to tips of toes.

- Knead muscles gently using your fingers and thumbs from top of thigh to ankle.

- Massage the ankle area following natural shapes with your palms or fingers.

- Using your thumbs massage the soles of the feet from heel to toe.

- Stroke each toe individually.

## The stomach

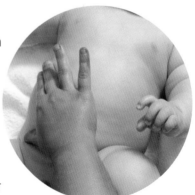

Gently massage the tummy in a clockwise direction around the belly button (navel), moving from your left to right. This stroke follows the natural direction of the large bowel.

Note
This stroke and the chest stroke for the diaphragm can be particularly useful if your toddler has a sore tummy or is constipated.

## The chest

- Starting at the centre front of the chest and using both hands stroke in a down and out direction following the spaces between the ribs. This strokes the small muscles running between the ribs used for breathing.

- Starting at the centre front of the chest where the ribs meet at the lower end of the breastbone, using both thumbs, stroke down and out following the line of the bottom rib. This follows the line of the big breathing muscle or diaphragm.

Note
These strokes can be particularly useful if your toddler suffers from 'wheeziness' or 'chestiness'.

## The arms

- Stroke from shoulder to fingertips.

- Knead muscles gently using your fingers and thumb from top of arm to wrist.

- Massage wrist using thumb and forefinger.

- Stroke the back of hands using fingers.

- Knead the palm of the hand using your thumbs.

- Stroke each finger using your fingertips and thumb.

Note
While working on his hands encourage your toddler to look at what you are doing and count each finger.

173

## The head (Use no oil)

- Stroke around the top of the head using palms or fingers.
- Stroke down the sides of the face using fingertips.

## The face (Use no oil)

Using fingertips stroke:

- From the centre of the forehead to the temples.
- In circles on the temples.
- Eyebrows from nose to temple.
- From nose over cheeks to ears.
- From inner corners of eyes down sides of nose to corners of mouth.
- From centre of chin out to the ears.
- Behind the ears from top to bottom.
- The ears back and front, following their shape.

## The neck

Stroke in a downward direction from:

- Ears to shoulders.
- Chin to upper chest.

## The whole front

- Using both hands, one for each half of the body, stroke from neck to toes including arms.

## The back of the body

- If your toddler does not want to lie on his tummy do these strokes with him across your lap or over your shoulder.

### Head (Use no oil)

- Using fingers and palms from top of head to base of skull.

## The neck and shoulders

Using fingertips gently massage muscles in a circular motion:

- From top to base of neck on either side of the spine.

- From neck out to shoulders.

## The back

From neck to buttocks:

- Using whole palm of hand stroke downwards.

- Using fingertips of both hands massage muscles in a descending circular fashion on either side of the spine.

## The legs

- Stroke legs from tops of thighs to toes.

### The whole back

- Give several long strokes from neck to ankle.

### To finish

- Wrap your toddler and cuddle him for a few minutes before starting the dressing process.

### Precautions

- Do not expect your toddler to sit still in one place for a period of time, make the most of opportunities to massage as they occur.

- Using oil makes toddlers very slippery so carefully choose the times you use it.

- Do not use oil on your toddler's skin before going outside because of the risk of sunburn.

- Do not extend massage time beyond the stage where either of you cease to enjoy it.

# benefits

- **Physical – Toning skin and muscles. Developing loving touch and body awareness. Promoting general body control through relaxation.**
- **Other – Enhancing parent/child relationship and learning stress management.**

# Action songs and rhymes

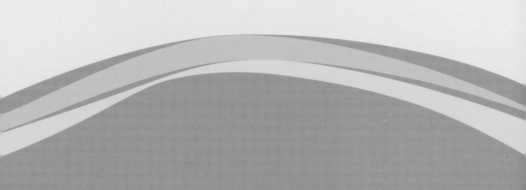

## Baa baa black sheep –
from page 24

Baa baa black sheep
Have you any wool?
Yes sir, yes sir, three bags full
One for the master and one
for the dame
And one for the little boy
who lives down the lane.

## Bell horses –
from page 63

Bell horses, bell horses
What time of day?
One o'clock, two o'clock
Three and away.
Bell horses, bell horses
What time of day?
Two o'clock, three o'clock
Four and away.
Bell horses, bell horses
What time of day?
Five o'clock, six o'clock
Now time to play.

## Clap, clap hands –
from page 38

Clap, clap hands, one,
two, three
Place your hands upon
your knee
Lift them high to touch the sky
Clap, clap hands and away
they fly.

## Dance to your daddy –
from page 168

Dance to your daddy,
my little babby

Dance to your daddy,
my little lamb.

You shall have a fishy
on a little dishy

You shall have a fishy,
when the boat comes in.

## Down at the station –
from page 165

Down at the station,
early in the morning

See the little puffer trains
all in a row.

See the engine driver
pull his little lever,

Puff, puff, peep, peep, off we go!

## Five currant buns –

from page 145

Five currant buns
in a baker's shop

Round and fat with sugar
on the top

Along came a boy with
a penny one day

Bought a currant bun
and took it away.

Repeat with: Four currant
buns etc.

## Five little ducks –

from page 61

Five little ducks went swimming
one day

Over the hills and far away

Mummy duck said 'quack quack
quack quack'

But only *four little ducks
came back

Repeat with *three, two, one

Last verse, last line – And all the
five little ducks came back.

## Five little monkeys –

from pages 127 and 136

Five little monkeys walked
along the shore

One went a-sailing

Then there were four

Four little monkeys climbed
up a tree

One of them tumbled down

Then there were three

Three little monkeys found
a pot of glue

One got stuck in it

Then there were two

Two little monkeys found
a currant bun

One ran away with it

Then there was one

One little monkey cried
all afternoon

So they put him in an aeroplane
and sent him to the moon!

## Grand old Duke of York –
from pages 100 and 159

The grand old Duke of York

He had ten thousand men

He marched them up
to the top of the hill

And he marched them
down again.

When they were up
they were up

And when they were
down they were down

But when they were
only halfway up

They were neither up nor down.

## Half a pound of
## tuppenny rice –
from page 88

Half a pound of tuppenny rice

Half a pound of treacle

Mix it up and make it nice

Pop goes the weasel.

## Head, shoulders,
## knees and toes –
from page 53

Head, shoulders, knees
and toes, knees and toes

Head, shoulders, knees
and toes, knees and toes

And eyes and ears
and mouth and nose

Head, shoulders, knees
and toes, knees and toes.

### Hey diddle diddle –
from page 54

Hey diddle diddle

The cat and the fiddle

The cow jumped over the moon

The little dog laughed

To see such fun

And the dish ran away with the spoon.

### Horsey horsey –
from page 165

Horsey horsey don't you stop

Just let your feet go clippety clop

The tail goes swish and the wheels go round

Giddy-up we're homeward bound.

### Hot cross buns –
from page 116

Hot cross buns

Hot cross buns

One a-penny, two a-penny

Hot cross buns.

## Humpty Dumpty –
from page 37

Humpty Dumpty sat on a wall

Humpty Dumpty had a great fall

All the king's horses and all
the king's men

Couldn't put Humpty
together again.

## Hush-a-bye baby –
from page 143

Hush-a-bye baby thy cradle
is green

Father's a nobleman, mother's
a queen

Betty's a lady and wears
a gold ring

John is a drummer and
plays for the king

Boom tiddy boom tiddy
boom boom boom.

## I had a little cherry stone –
from page 149

I had a little cherry stone

And put it in the ground

And when next year I went
to look

A tiny shoot I found

The shoot grew upwards
day by day

And soon became a tree

I picked the rosy cherries then

And ate them for my tea.

## I have a little garden –

from page 149

I have a little garden
Where I like to go
And that is where
All the red poppies grow
Repeat with:
Blue bells
Green grass
Yellow buttercups.

## I hear thunder –

from page 74

I hear thunder, I hear thunder
(drum feet on floor)
Hark don't you? Hark don't you?
(Pretend to listen)
Pitter patter raindrops
Pitter patter raindrops
I'm wet through
(shake body vigorously)
So are you
(point to friend).

## I love little kitty –
from page 107

I love little kitty, her coat
is so warm

And if I don't hurt her
she'll do me no harm,

So I'll not pull her tail,
nor drive her away

But kitty and I very
gently will play.

## I'm a little teapot –
from page 153

I'm a little teapot

Short and stout

Here's my handle

Here's my spout

When the tea is ready

Hear me shout – tip me
up and pour me out.

## Incy wincy spider –
from page 121

Incy wincy spider

Climbed up the spout

Down came the rain

And washed the spider out

Out came the sunshine

Dried up all the rain

Incy wincy spider climbed
up the spout again.

### Jack and Jill –
from pages 44 and 76

Jack and Jill went up the hill
To fetch a pail of water
Jack fell down
And broke his crown
And Jill came tumbling after.

### Jack be nimble –
from page 134

Jack be nimble, Jack be quick
Jack jump over the candlestick

### Jelly on a plate –
from page 34

Jelly on a plate
Jelly on a plate
Wibble wobble
Wibble wobble
Jelly on a plate.

### Jeremiah blow –
from page 80

Jeremiah, blow the fire
Puff, puff, puff
First you blow it gently
Then you blow it rough.

## Old King Cole –

from page 92

Old King Cole was a merry old soul

And a merry old soul was he.

He called for his pipe and he called for his bowl

And he called for his fiddlers three.

## One little baby rocking in a tree –

from page 102

One little baby rocking in a tree

Two little babies, splashing in the sea

Three little babies crawling on the floor

Four little babies banging on the door

Five little babies playing hide and seek

Keep your eyes tight closed now, until I say … peek!

## One man went to mow –

from page 58

One man went to mow

Went to mow a meadow

One man and his dog

Went to mow a meadow.

Repeat using two, three and so on, up to ten.

## One potato, two potato –
from page 132

One potato, two potato,
three potato, four

Five potato, six potato,
seven potato more.

## One two three a-leery –
from page 84

One two three a-leery

Four five six a-leery

Seven eight nine a-leery

Ten a-leery, watch me.

## One two three four five –
from page 31

One two three four five

Once I caught a fish alive

Six seven eight nine ten

Then I let it go again.

## Pat-a-cake –
from page 116

Pat-a-cake, pat-a-cake,
baker's man

Bake me a cake
as fast as you can

Pat it and prick it

And mark it with 'B'

Put it in the oven
for baby and me.

## Peter rabbit –
from page 124

(sing to the tune of
'John Brown's body')

Little Peter rabbit's got
a fly upon his nose x 3

(touch your baby's nose
on the word 'nose')

He swished it

(swipe with right hand
in front of your face)

And he swashed it

(swipe with left hand
in front of your face)

And the fly flew away

(flap your hands)

Floppy ears and
curly whiskers x 3

(hands sticking up from
your head like rabbits' ears,

then stroke imaginary whiskers
in circular motion)

And he swished it and
he swashed it

And the fly flew away.

(actions as above).

### Pussy cat pussy cat –
from page 140

Pussy cat pussy cat
Where have you been?
I've been to London
To visit the queen
Pussy cat pussy cat
What did you do there?
I frightened a little mouse
Under her chair.

### Ride a cock-horse –
from page 70

Ride a cock-horse
to Banbury Cross
To see a fine lady upon
a white horse
With rings on her fingers
and bells on her toes
She shall have music
wherever she goes.

### Ring a ring o'roses –
from page 23

Ring a ring o'roses
A pocketful of posies
Atishoo atishoo
We all fall down.

### Roses are red –
from page 110

Roses are red, violets
are blue
Sugar is sweet and so
are you.

### Sally go round –
from page 87

Sally go round the sun
Sally go round the moon
Sally go round the chimney pots
On a Saturday afternoon.

### Sing a song of sixpence –
from page 88

Sing a song of sixpence
A pocketful of rye
Four and twenty blackbirds
Baked in a pie
When the pie was opened
The birds began to sing
Wasn't that a dainty dish
To set before the king.

## Slip one and two –
from page 73

Slip one and two

Jump three and four

Turn around swiftly

And sit upon the floor

Clap one and two

Nod three and four

Jump up again

And be ready for more.

## Ten fat sausages –
from page 32

Ten fat sausages sitting in a pan

One went 'pop' another went 'bang'

Eight fat sausages, and so on

Last line: No fat sausages sitting in a pan.

## Ten green bottles –
from page 146

Ten green bottles hanging on the wall

Ten green bottles hanging on the wall

And if one green bottle should accidentally fall

There'd be nine green bottles hanging on the wall.

Repeat with: Nine, eight, seven, and so on.

## Ten in the bed –
from page 123

There were ten in the bed

And the little one said

Roll over! Roll over!

So they all rolled over

And one fell out ...

There were nine in the bed,
and so on down to one.

There was one in the bed

And the little one said

Roll over! Roll over!

So he rolled right over
and fell right out

There were none in the bed

So no one said

Roll over! Roll over!

## The doughnut song –
from page 145

I went to the baker's
to get something to eat

I felt so hungry from
my head to my feet

(gently pat head then feet)

So I picked up the doughnut
and wiped off the grease

And handed the lady
a penny piece

Well she looked at the penny
Then she looked at me

She said 'kind sir you
can plainly see'

'There's a hole in your penny,
there's a hole right through'

(peek through hole made
in your hands)

Says I, 'There's a hole
in your doughnut too!'

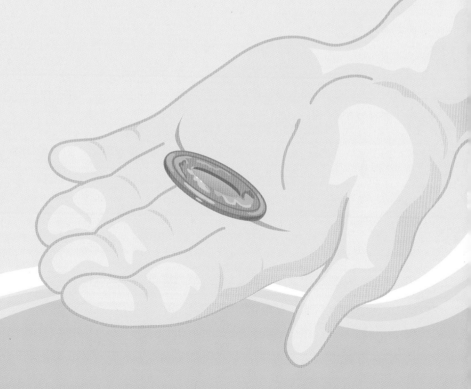

## The wheels on the bus –
from page 115

The wheels on the bus go round and round

Round and round, round and round

The wheels on the bus go round and round

All day long.

Repeat, changing to:

The horn on the bus goes toot toot toot.

The wipers ...go swish swish swish.

The people ...go up and down.

The driver ...goes broom broom broom.

## Three little speckled frogs
– from page 166

Three little speckled frogs

Sat on a speckled log

Eating the most delicious grubs (yum yum)

One jumped into the pool

Where it was nice and cool

Then there were two speckled frogs.

Repeat with:

Two, one and finish with:

Then there were no speckled frogs.

## Three tiny kittens –
from page 130

Three tiny kittens

Climb up a tree

See them jump down again

One, two, three.

## To market, to market –
from page 96

To market, to market, to buy
a fat pig

Home again, home again,
jiggety jig.

To market, to market, to buy
a fat hog

Home again, home again,
jiggety jog.

## Tommy Thumb –
from page 79

Tommy Thumb, Tommy Thumb

Where are you?

Here I am, here I am

How do you do.

Repeat with:

Peter Pointer, Toby Tall, Ruby
Ring, Baby Small, Fingers All.

## Two little dicky birds –
from pages 46 and 124

Two little dicky birds

Sitting on a wall

One named Peter, the other
named Paul

Fly away Peter

Fly away Paul

Come back Peter

Come back Paul.

## Two little feet –
from page 119

Two little feet go tap tap tap

Two little hands go clap clap
clap

Two little eyes open wide

One little head wags from
side to side.